AF270656

NIKE

KENNY ABDO

Fly!
An Imprint of Abdo Zoom
abdobooks.com

abdobooks.com

Published by Abdo Zoom, a division of ABDO, P.O. Box 398166, Minneapolis, Minnesota 55439. Copyright © 2023 by Abdo Consulting Group, Inc. International copyrights reserved in all countries. No part of this book may be reproduced in any form without written permission from the publisher. Fly!™ is a trademark and logo of Abdo Zoom.

Printed in the United States of America, North Mankato, Minnesota.
052022
092022

Photo Credits: Alamy, AP Images, Getty Images, Shutterstock
Production Contributors: Kenny Abdo, Jennie Forsberg, Grace Hansen
Design Contributors: Candice Keimig, Neil Klinepier, Laura Graphenteen

Library of Congress Control Number: 2021950291

Publisher's Cataloging-in-Publication Data

Names: Abdo, Kenny, author.
Title: Nike / by Kenny Abdo.
Description: Minneapolis, Minnesota : Abdo Zoom, 2023 | Series: Hype brands |
    Includes online resources and index.
Identifiers: ISBN 9781098228545 (lib. bdg.) | ISBN 9781644947975 (pbk.) |
    ISBN 9781098229382 (ebook) | ISBN 9781098229801 (Read-to-Me ebook)
Subjects: LCSH: Clothing and dress--Juvenile literature. | Brand name products--
    Juvenile literature. | Nike (Firm)--Juvenile literature. | Fashion--Social aspects--
    Juvenile literature. | Sport clothes industry--Juvenile literature. | Popular culture--
    Juvenile literature.
Classification: DDC 338.7--dc23

TABLE OF CONTENTS

NIKE

While Nike is known mostly in the athletics world, the brand still goes hand in hand with hype culture!

From being sold out of a car trunk to becoming a **streetwear** giant, Nike's "swoosh" can be heard around the world!

HYPE

In 1964, track athlete Philip Knight and his coach Bill Bowerman set up a small business together. They **imported** Japanese running shoes and called it Blue Ribbon Sports (BRS).

9

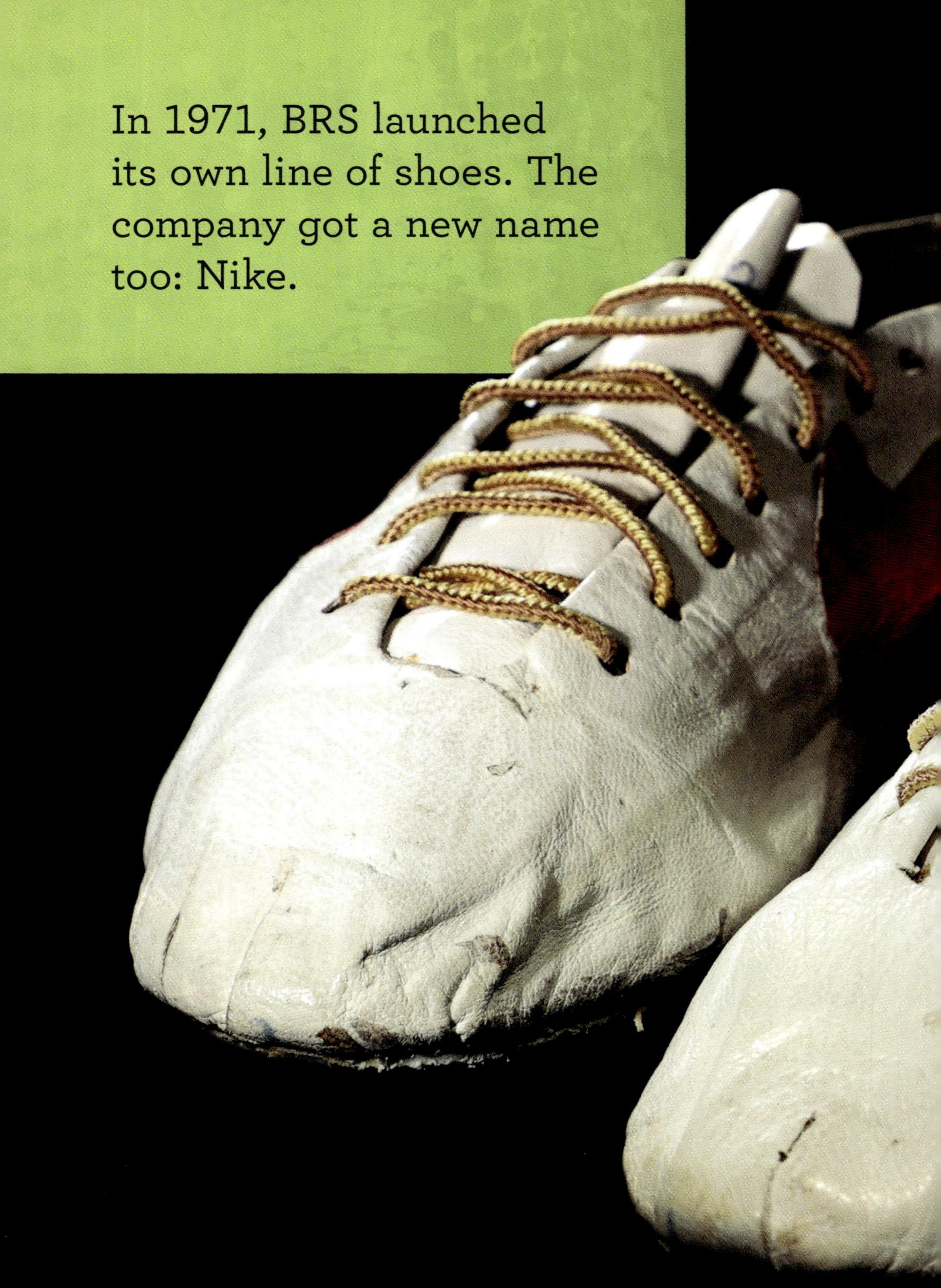

In 1971, BRS launched its own line of shoes. The company got a new name too: Nike.

Graphic designer Carolyn Davidson created the famous "swoosh" logo. She earned $35 for her creation, not knowing it would become recognized around the world.

Through the 80s and 90s, Nike ruled the athletic footwear market. The company wanted to expand its reach with other products.

ALL THE RAGE

In the late 1990s, Nike shoes began being mixed with other fashion styles. Combining sneakers with preppy clothes created a unique look!

By the late 2000s, Nike Elite socks became fashionable with star athletes. Hip-hop **influencers** took notice and began wearing them, too!

In 2014, Nike introduced a new line. NikeLab focused more on **streetwear** than sportswear.

In 2017, Nike **collaborated** with Off-White. Their sneakers became a must-have for all hype-hungry celebrities, from Justin Bieber to David Beckham!

In 2019, someone paid $400,000 for a pair of 1972 Moon Shoes at an **auction**! A pair of Michael Jordan's 1984 Air Ships sold for a record $1.5M in 2021!

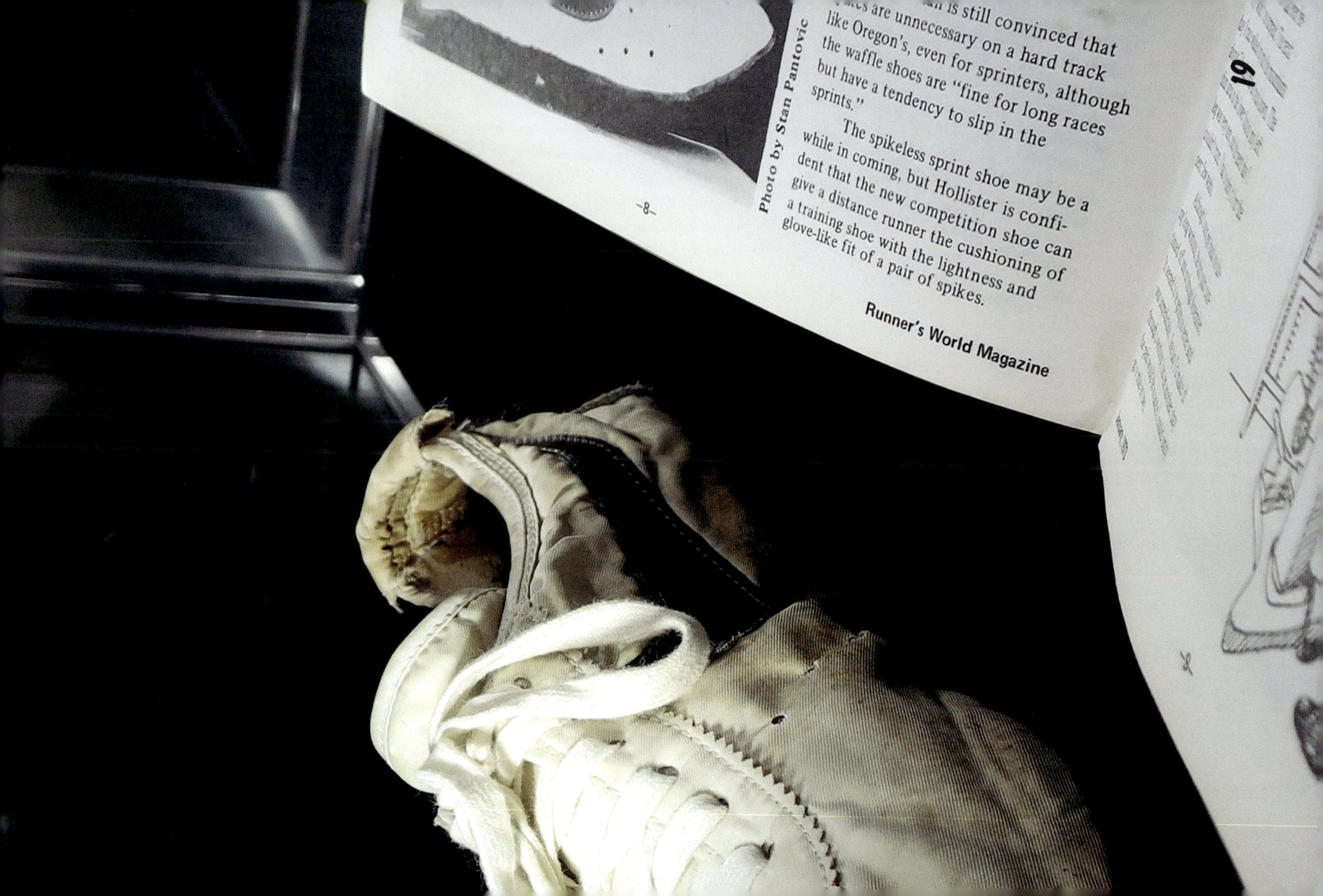
is still convinced that
like Oregon's, even for sprinters, although
the waffle shoes are "fine for long races
but have a tendency to slip in the
sprints."
The spikeless sprint shoe may be a
while in coming, but Hollister is confi-
dent that the new competition shoe can
give a distance runner the cushioning of
a training shoe with the lightness and
glove-like fit of a pair of spikes.
Runner's World Magazine
Photo by Stan Pantovic
19

In 2021, Nike released the SNKRS app. It lets customers bid for the newest and rarest shoes as soon as they **drop**.

With celebrity **endorsements**, slick designs, and constant alterations, the "swoosh" will always hover at the top of the sports and street style games!

GLOSSARY

auction – a sale at which goods are sold to the highest bidder.

collaborate – to work with another person or group in order to do something or reach a goal.

drop – when something that is highly anticipated is released to the public.

endorse – the act of publicly recommending a product or service in exchange for money.

import – to bring in goods from another country for sale or use.

influencer – a person who has a large following on their social media accounts and can persuade their audience to buy certain products or services.

streetwear – fashionable, yet casual clothing worn by followers of popular culture. It is heavily influenced by hip-hop and surf culture.

ONLINE RESOURCES

Booklinks
NONFICTION NETWORK
FREE! ONLINE NONFICTION RESOURCES

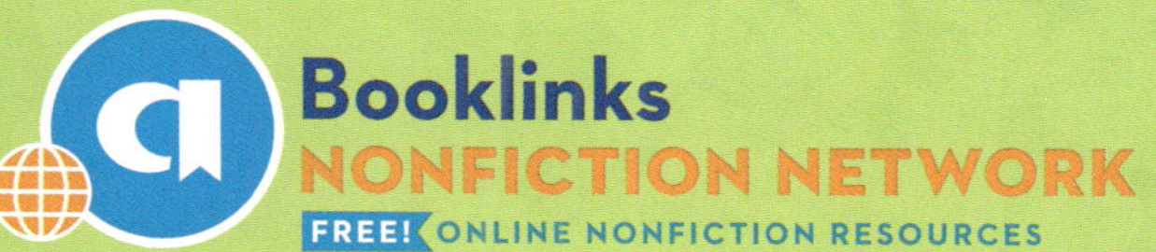

To learn more about Nike, please visit **abdobooklinks.com** or scan this QR code. These links are routinely monitored and updated to provide the most current information available.

INDEX